Seventh-day Adventists Interpreting Scripture and Establishing Fundamental Doctrines

Edward W. H. Vick

Energion Publications
Gonzalez, Florida, USA
February, 2020

Copyright © 2020, Edward W. H. Vick
All Rights Reserved

ISBN: 978-1-63199-431-9
eISBN: 978-1-63199-433-3

Energion Publications
P. O. Box 841
Gonzalez, Florida 32533

energion.com

Peace be with you......Breathe deeply and slowly now...its OK.
Smile, smile now and think a good thought.
It will push all the bad thoughts away.
Make the effort to smile and think a good thought.

It is like going to the gym and working your muscles.
This is the good mind gym and you have to physically smile,
and be thankful for something good.
Anything good, like you have the eyes to read this.
You have the equipment to read this on.

There is always something good for you to be thankful for sweetheart,
and then you are training your life to be better for you.

Because with good thoughts comes a better life.

....to keep talking about all the bad stuff creates more of the same my dear.....
So, please try to smile, and be thankful you have read this message now.....
It will save your life.....
Peace be with you and have a good evening now.
.
.
.
Smile,
Now you must think good... Light.... Thoughts.

Smile and love him.
Thank him.
Be friends with him.
Speak to him.
He is always with you.
Smile,
It is all good now.
.
.
.
Love,
Love yourself,
Love your family,
Love your life....
Smile, there, that's better.

Love them
Love yourself
Love your husband
Love
A small word,
A huge difference.

.
.
.
.

Here is an opportunity for you...
The book,
Christian Science by Mary Baker Eddy.
Take from it what you need.
There is a section on mental health treatment,
that requires your belief in perfection.

You keep telling him he is perfect,
His cells hear and remember perfection.
They get reprogramming from the words you speak.

So far, the cells have been programmed with disease!

He is perfect,
and your words and his own belief will create his wellness.

It is one path or the other.

Watch Forest Gump, his mother always believed in his perfection, and look how he turned out.

Don't forget...
Your belief in this disease is stronger than your belief in his perfection at this time...

When you believe he is perfect,
He will be.
Peace be with you and your child.

.
.
.
.

Smile,
Congratulations, you are learning not to judge.
You see yourself.
You hear yourself!

Yes, you hear you!
Now, love yourself and wish yourself only the very best.
And be thankful, for they teach you how you can succeed.

Love yourself and you rise up too!
.
.
.
Love him any way...
That love makes you feel better.
Physical Contact is not love.
Love feels good.
It is the love you feel for yourself that feels good.

Look at you.
Love you.
Hug you.
Love you.
.
.
.
Worrying is...
using your imagination to create something you don't want.
.
.
.
Smile,
Congratulations
He is your opposite so you could choose the path you wanted...
Or agree with what you didn't want.

Thank him for showing you the way.
Thank him for being your opposite so you could find your way.
Thank him.
He is your friend.
We all are.
.
.

step 1....ASK.
step 2....Smile, feel good and Love the steps.
step 3....Keep going.
step 4....Be thankful for the strength to keep going.
....and keep Smiling all the way to the top!
.
.
.
.
...Its is never too late......Peace be with you
.
.
.
..
Why do you want to stop feeling that?
It is energy,
and it is doing what energy does best...
Keeping you alive...
Peace be with you .
.
.
.
.
Read solutions....
to get you out of the level of questioning.
Peace be with you
.
.
.
.
You feel an overwhelming sense of Peace and Love for others who are unkind to you....
You smile sweetly at them, and love them anyway.
Peace be with you too
.
.
.
.
Life is good.....Peace be with you too
.
.
.
.

Preface

Here is an interesting account of how from the early days, the mid nineteenth century in Eastern America, a particular community came into being through a series of quite unusual, not to say astonishing, experiences.

It focuses on one persisting group of believers, explaining how they interpreted a carefully selected set of Scriptures, and focuses on that unique method of interpreting Scripture. That was an inheritance they took over from the teaching of William Miller.

The overall theme in this short writing is that of interpretation. Frank discussion of the method of interpretation, hermeneutic, is of primary importance for any serious believer since the way you interpret Scripture determines how you will believe and act.

There are six chapters.

Chapter one traces the development of events, several disappointments and the course of interpretation to which they gave rise.

Chapter two details how the second stage developed with radical reinterpretation of key terms, 'sanctuary', 'cleansing' but retaining the hermeneutic method. The result was accepted as 'essential Adventism'

Chapter three sets out certain convictions now approved by the present conservative leadership of the Seventh-day Adventist church, to observers they are of special interest, and to the less traditional members appear as too easy, even dogmatic, acceptance of what has become Adventist tradition.

From 1843 to 2018, the method of interpretation inherited from Miller has persisted among Adventists and produced the unique clams its members make for the church. Some of these are detailed in this chapter. The present leadership likes tradition.

Chapter four invites the reader to go back to the Gospels.

Chapter five examines the meaning of Ellen White's claim to be the lesser light in relation to the greater light, the Scriptures.

Chapter six presents and explains Hiram Edson' s contribution to the developing community.

Table of Contents

	Preface iii
I	Early Experiences: Establishing Essential Doctrines 1
II	Adventist Hermeneutic 27
III	How to Understand an Adventist 37
IV	Back to the Gospels 45
V	Lesser Light To Greater Light...55
VI	Edson's Hypothesis 63

I Early Experiences
The story of essential Adventism

01 HERMENEUTIC FOR AN EMERGING COMMUNITY

(1) The method of interpreting Scripture with a view to produce doctrine is an exercise called 'hermeneutic'.

We might distinguish 'exegesis'. This is the study of the scriptural text. It may or may not be employed in the service of developing doctrine.

(2) As the Adventist community developed after 1844, it continued to employ a hermeneutic that produced a set of doctrines that were to define the group.

(3) That hermeneutic served to strengthen the convictions and the beliefs held already, and provided for those that the community would embrace. One of these is the overall conviction that they were being led by God, even if making mistakes in the process of development that led to errors of belief and of judgment. Their hermeneutic led them to find unique applications of Scripture.

Examples are found in the interpretation of the parable of the virgins to fit their recent experience and Hiram Edson's unexpected inferences from *Leviticus* 26.

(4) For these disappointed Millerites, the results of this interpretation of Scripture produced very welcome teachings. These results confirmed for them that their method of interpretation was correct and unassailable. Consensus emerged with the firm belief that honest discussion was always appropriate, until they achieved a broad agreement.

02 THE DOCTRINAL PRODUCT

As they developed, it became clear that a new community was emerging with a set of unique doctrines that set them apart from all other Christian communities. This separation was underwritten by energetic assertions that they had a mission to tell the world of the judgment of God, and the soon coming of the end. That became their unique message and provided them with their unique task. They believed that the fact that a distinctive community was emerging was evidence for divine guidance and for the correctness of their interpretations of Scripture. That leads to the question, Is it correct to assume that the success of the emerging community, the Advent Movement, demonstrates the correctness of the hermeneutic, as well as the truth of the doctrines it produced, i. e. a doctrine of God's judgment, with predictions about its execution in the last day final events, and the divine guidance in the process of deriving these teachings?

Convinced as they were, that conviction was strengthened with the surprising success they achieved as they continued to preach. They did not ask the question, 'What are we to make of the doctrines that this method of literalistic prophetic interpretation produces?' For even today the community that developed over time holds fast in its authoritarian pronouncements to the fundamentalist prophetic interpretation of Scripture. What results is an unquestioning attitude on the part of the faithful to the results of the hermeneutic: a doctrine of God's judgment and predictions about its execution in the last day events.

The point is that it is essential to examine, that is to say to question the status of the doctrine which emerges. That hermeneutic led to the doctrine of God's judgment as the basic theme. Is it reasonable to question the doctrine that emerged?

That would also mean that we must question the way in which that teaching is arrived at. If we question the way in which that conclusion was reached we must also give serious critical attention to the hermeneutic that produced it.

We cannot relate to our past unless we know enough about that past to enable us to make constructive judgments about that past. Only then may we make satisfactory judgments about our present relations both to that past and to the present. The Advent Movement made its appearance and developed its teachings and policies in a world very different from our world. Their world, now nearly two centuries away, was in fact one of several worlds in the eastern United States. Their attitudes firmly held were very different from ours. That 'world' was one where persuasive predictions about the end of the world met with largely uncritical but enthusiastic response by large numbers of people. This involved the making and acceptance of predictions based on the unique interpretation of carefully selected biblical passages, according to a unique method of interpretation of Scripture which carried conviction to receptive listeners. The method and the results, being accepted with enthusiastic relief, came to be taken for granted. Accepting the assumptions and the arguments presented to develop those assumptions seemed most reasonable, and so the end of the world was expected with certainty.

What enabled the making and acceptance of predictions of such consequence was a specific attitude to Scripture. Start with the (1) the conviction that Scripture has a particular and unique status, i.e. a special kind of authority and (2) accept the assumptions and the logic of the persuasive Millerite rite preaching that prediction is certain of fulfillment when attention and direction is given to particular passages, so that its prophecies can be understood. This involved (3) a unique method of interpreting Scripture.

But when and since the prediction was not fulfilled, each of these convictions needed re-examining.

03 APPEAL TO SELECTED APOCALYPTIC PASSAGES

The hermeneutic that grounded this system restricted appeal to varied but limited texts of Scripture. Dominant was the appeal to apocalyptic passages, *Leviticus*, *Daniel*, passages from the Gospels, e.g. *Matthew 24*, *Revelation*. Since a guiding focus was the activity of the ancient Hebrew tabernacle, the sanctuary, mention of the concept of 'sanctuary' in the rare passages in the New Testament, e.g. in the book of *Hebrews*, were assessed and taken to refer to actual events in the heavenly sphere. So the Old Testament book of *Leviticus*, with detailed account of the procedures in the tabernacle became essential to the doctrinal system that was developing. The theme was limited. The sanctuary doctrine became the central focus and interest. Isolated as that focus was, it led to the isolation of the community that produced and preached it. That community indeed embraced the isolation, often in polemic ways. Later it claimed that it was the true church, the 'remnant' and alone possessed the truth for the last days. Indeed to embrace the teaching and become a member of the community was described as 'accepting the truth', 'coming into the truth'.

04 WHY THE NOTION OF 'SANCTUARY' BECAME CENTRAL.

The answer is fourfold. First, it enabled the Advent Movement to hold on to the prophetic method of interpreting Scripture. Second, it provided it with a convincing account of why the Millerite conclusion was an error. Third, it made it possible for them to build and exist as a new community. Fourth, it gave it scriptural authority for claiming divine guidance for their very existence as a movement.

The idea of sanctuary as indicating activity of the divine in the heavens came to Hiram Edson the day after the disappointment October 23, 1844. Upset and baffled by the non-occurrence of the great consummation expected on the preceding day but disappointed, it came as a great relief, when the idea occurred to him that the sanctuary, which Miller identified as the earth, was located as a reality, a literal, physical reality in the heavens. That idea was eagerly welcomed by a frustrated group. Disappointed by the failure of Miller's predictions about October 22 1844, it readily accepted the hypothesis of Edson. What was of little interest to it and hardly noticed was that while Miller's claim could be and was shown to be an error by events, in his case a grand non-event, Edson's claim could not be verified. There is no way of testing the existence or activity of divine agents in the heavens. So there is no way of showing the doctrine to be either true or false. It was a venture into belief, a speculation.

The heavenly sanctuary was seen as fulfillment of the prototypal system of Old Testament times, and as such was believed to be quite literal. For, having completed the activity in the heavenly sanctuary, the claim was made that Christ will come to earth, to execute final judgment. The *parousia* takes place. But that is in the future. The advent will be 'soon' but paradoxically we cannot say when! So we cannot, indeed must not, give the term 'soon' any temporal content.

The theme developed into a complicated set of claims. The framers of the new teaching called upon an elaborate and extensive set of parallels from the ancient Israelite tabernacle to provide the basis. To this were added statements from the book of Revelation about the final judgment that served to connect the post-1844 turbulent times within the emerging community with the Second Advent and the redemption and destruction that had so agitated Miller and his followers. That Final Judgment meant redemption for the righteous which included the 'remnant', and the final universal destruction of the unrighteous.

Different groups moved in different directions following the disappointment of their deeply cherished hopes. We have described the course which the 'Advent Movement' took. This developed into the Seventh-day Adventist Church. Here insistence on the sacredness of the seventh day Sabbath and the obligation to keep it holy added a further separating feature and emphasised the isolation of the community from other bodies in the Christian community. This was embraced by the emerging community. Indeed it became an essential part of its message for the world. 'We are unique in our teaching. We are unique in that our reason for existing is to provide the world with the opportunity to accept our message while opportunity remains in these last days before the Final Judgment'. This was its astonishing conclusion.

05 THE PROPHETIC HERMENEUTIC IS RETAINED AFTER THE DISAPPOINTMENT

After the Disappointment, some of the disappointed believers continued their firm belief in divine guidance, even if the result turned out to be unexpected and the prediction in error.

This raises a serious question. Does divine guidance lead into error? It is a question that may be raised about later developments. Does God guide you, when knowing he leads you to a false conclusion?

Even if questions were raised about the validity of the hermeneutic that produced conclusions and actions based on those conclusions, what became the 'Advent Movement' decided that it must continue to employ the same method of interpretation that had produced the Great Disappointment. It had no desire and hence no incentive seriously to question the way they were interpreting and using Scripture. Their belief was that God had been and was still guiding them in that use. Hence it continued in its enthusiastic application.

06 SERIOUS STUDY OF SCRIPTURE ELSEWHERE

Beginning in the eighteenth century and, blossoming in the nineteenth, came the so-called 'critical' study of Scripture, opening up new questions and new and extensive research into the composition and history of the Bible. The aim was to understand the diverse literature within its various contexts and according to its genre. In practice this involves treating the biblical writings as other literary writings were being treated.

That serious work required expert knowledge of history, of original languages, of how manuscripts were discovered and compared so that a correct text might emerge, how manuscripts were transmitted and preserved and why there were differences in the texts of various copies. It involved first the recognition and then the examination of different genres of writing e.g. wisdom, apocalyptic, legal, and historical. The Hebrew Scriptures were called 'law, prophets and writings'. It also led to the comparison of biblical stories with those of cultures other than the Hebrew, in particular those of the origin of the cosmos, creation stories, and sagas of a widespread flood. Research and debate continued and still continues in the search for the best possible explanations of the original composition of Scripture.

So we have two approaches that should not be set in opposition. Ordinary believers can read the Bible and find truth, meaning, comfort and challenge in that reading as the original translators intended. They find it to be the medium of God's revelation, the gateway to Christian faith and to its nurture. The scholars, whose dedicated lives were devoted to answering serious questions about Scripture, provided results that are by nature academic. But that by no means need result in opposition between their Bible and the Bible of the ordinary believer. Quite the contrary! It provides for new understanding, and is readily accessible to all serious believers.

The Reformation led to a widespread change of attitude to the Scriptures. No longer was the Scripture locked away in a language known only to the clergy and the scholar. At great cost and sacrifice and assisted by the activity of the recently developed printed press, it became accessible to the ordinary believer.

The simple believer, who now had the opportunity to read Scripture, might readily understand that there was no need for the church's intervention to mediate salvation and provide forgiveness, absolution and indulgences. But this questioning of its established authority led the church to respond ruthlessly with a bitter, violent and continued reaction.

Take the case of Tyndale and his struggle to the death to make the Scriptures available to all readers. He was a robust, fearless, brilliant and dedicated scholar. His work in translating the Bible into English provided the translators of the King James Version with a very large percentage of its content. He had one most worthy and very simple incentive. He wanted the ploughboy to be able to read and to understand Scripture without the intervention of the clergy who for years were the only ones who had access to the words of Scripture. They read Latin. Scripture was in Latin, the language of the Vulgate version.

The reformers insisted that ordinary believers could understand the message of Scripture if they had the chance of reading it in their language. That provided Luther with the incentive to render Scripture into German as it did for Tyndale to translate it into English.

07 IMPORTANT TERMS EXPLAINED

It is most unfortunate that the word 'criticism' has become such a negative, even taboo, word for fundamentalists. Certainly the term 'criticism' often carries negative overtones. We often use the term when we have disagreements, or reservations. But it also has a positive connotation.

In the context of biblical studies, it simply means careful, serious approach and examination of the available materials. If you take the term 'criticism' to have only negative meaning, then you will have a prejudice against the use of it in the context of Christian biblical studies where it is meant to affirm dedicated and disciplined attitudes and procedures for the understanding of the body of writing we call Scripture.

Here we speak of 'higher' and 'lower' criticism. That needs a little explanation. Within fundamentalist circles it is almost exclusively the 'higher' criticism that comes in for negative treatment. For, it is the conclusions of this method that conservative Christians do not like. Dissatisfaction with these conclusions is then extended to the method that suggested them. So, both are rejected. If they disagree about date, composition, authorship along with other conclusions, they do not engage in an attempt to provide reasons for alternatives, but rather proceed to reject the method of the 'higher criticism' that has produced the unwelcome positions.

The terms 'higher' and 'lower' are here being used allegorically. Their context is of a flowing body of water, a river and its source. It is not at all a reference to altitude (how could it be in this context?) nor to scale of value. It refers to the flowing of the water from source to final outlet. Nearer the source we are further 'up' indeed 'higher up' stream. Further downstream we are 'lower' i. e. further 'down' in the process.

So think of Scripture as like a river. The words and sentences and chapters and 'books', as we call them, have a history. There was a time when they did not exist. There were none at all. There was a time when they began to emerge and to be put into written form. 'Higher' up in the process we are thinking of the emerging of the material that will later be written down and later still be recognised as important.

Apply this to the New Testament. For the earliest Christians a 'holy' book had not yet emerged. Writings were eventually produced, saved and treasured. We call them 'books' but that could be misleading. There was a time when there was no New Testament. Some of these books were compiled before others, coming from different sources. Ask the question about their sources, i.e. about what happened higher upstream. What is the date and context of the writings? How to account for repetitions and duplications of the text? Are there multiple sources of the resulting text? When you have a book in your hand with the accepted text, you can then also ask about what happened lower downstream. For example, such questions as: What do we know about the different versions and what is their significance? Which is the best reading, the one which gets us closer to the 'author'? So asks the 'lower' criticism, as it works with a text already formed.

The conservative attitude to Scripture is often ready to ignore such questions, even if they assume that the version they are reading is acceptable. That version will not be in the original language of Scripture. So we have the further kind of question to ask. This concerns whether the translation is faithful to the original and provides the best rendering of the meaning of the original. Without some knowledge of the original language the reader has no alternative but to assume that his text is reliable.

Fundamentalists treat all Scripture as equally authoritative when asserting the inspiration of the chosen writings. That means that any text taken from anywhere can be linked with other texts and these taken as proof texts for developing a doctrine; often simply ignoring and not investigating the text in its original context. That becomes a secondary issue. To be neutral regarding the context of the text leads to the conclusion that the proof texts that emerge are all equal in importance in contributing to the construction of a doctrine. That is a mistake in the interpretation of Scripture. 'A text without context is a pretext for proof texts'. The conservative must ask seriously whether it is not a serious distortion of acceptable procedure of biblical interpretation to ignore context for the sake of building a system of doctrine That the results may be welcome is beside the point.

08 ADVENTIST ATTITUDES

The following attitudes: emerged as Adventism developed:

(1) In developing doctrine from the text of Scripture, do not ask questions like the following: proper procedure for establishing the date of the composition of the book, how the final text was compiled into 'books', what the relation is between passages which are duplicated within and between the books, how different versions of events are found in the individual books, etc.

(2) Treat all passages of Scripture as of equal value as sources of doctrine. But overlook passages considered irrelevant

(3) Accept the text as it stands, treating passages from any biblical book as divinely inspired message from God, and take them literally. Any chosen passage has an equal status with any other chosen passage, and all can be used as 'proof texts'.

(4) Attempt, where appropriate, to co-ordinate the text of Scripture with future events and so make predictions about that future, even specifying dates or periods of time in relation to those future events. This became a dominating concern. So much is this the case that the term 'Voice of Prophecy' became a designation for the movement. 'We are unique in that we have the God-given mission to foretell for you the future of the world and of God's activity of judgment in relation to its inhabitants. That is our unique responsibility and defines our existence. That makes us quite unique.'

09 PRINCIPLES OF INTERPRETATION

The sanctuary idea occupied a great deal of interest and it became the central theme for extended development, becoming an elaborate as well as an essential doctrine. Inherited from William Miller, it was duly modified at the suggestion of Hiram Edson and has been modified again as time has passed. The context has changed quite radically and so has its meaning. For Miller it signified Advent, final judgment and world destruction at a particular year, month and day.

For Adventists, with the modified adjustment, the idea of the sanctuary enabled them to make claims about atonement, mediation, judgment as inquiry, and judgment as execution. Adventists insisted on

(1) retaining the primary importance of the basic idea of sanctuary.

(2) retaining the hermeneutic of prophetic interpretation,

(3) retaining the doctrine produced by that hermeneutic, even if the doctrine has been altered beyond the initial teaching. So now a different story is being told.

But a serious and very basic question has remained unexamined and unanswered, reflecting a non-theological attitude to the discussion. Do not ask seriously and critically what sort of God, what doctrine of God, the story demands. The doctrine says that God will punish the non-saved by killing them twice, once at the start of the millennium, and then after having raised them for the purpose, kill them again at the final judgment of the unrighteous. By adding complicated details, we end up at the end of all things earthly. That was the point where Miller ended his story! But here we have much detail.

If the exegesis of Scripture leads to such a doctrine of God's justice, it must be in error, in application or in principle or both.

For one example of the lengths they were prepared to go to maintain the rightness of the course their history was taking, and to maintain their beliefs and convictions take the example of the interpretation of the parable of the virgins, where every detail of the parable is seen to fit the details of their recent experience following the Great Disappointment.

For another see Edson's treatment of the passage in *Leviticus* 26, where he finds confirmation of his claim about a date, A. D. 1798, and an event, centuries in advance of the context of scriptural passages. He then identifies that date as the beginning of the end.

What they claimed was the following:

This is the way we interpret Scripture.

These are the results we get.

The results we get confirm the correctness of our method of interpretation, of our assumptions, beliefs, convictions and conclusions.

This claim is made that even if there is no way to confirm the results, for example that there is a universe of created beings in a celestial realm beyond our reach, some good and some rebellious, to whom God is revealing his justice. Those results are assured, for we are dealing with 'the more sure word of prophecy. We are in fact the 'Voice of Prophecy'.

All of this and more represents the heritage of current Adventist positions regarding both hermeneutic and doctrine.

010 THE FOUNDATION OF THE ARGUMENT AND THE STEPS IN IT

The application of the term 'day' to represent a literal year becomes the key, to be applied to all prophetic passages where the term 'day' features. What follows that original occurrence is the speculation that the principle is to be applied to all prophetic passages where the mention of time occurs. Since this is crucial as the primary clue for interpretation, we look more closely at the original occurrence, where the idea features. The Scriptural writings were inspired and authoritative as other writings were. But they were mysterious and so to be properly understood they needed a clue as to how they should be interpreted.

In that original context what is in view is punishment of Israel and Jerusalem for their iniquities. Here the texts are referring to corporate entities, nations and empires. It is to be noted that other corporate entities beside Israel and Judah are also the subject of prophetic announcements in Scripture: for example, Egypt, Assyria, Babylon.

One spokesman is the prophet Ezekiel. He is to represent visually the coming of judgment, the literal desolation of Israel and Jerusalem. He is to do this by performing unusual acts to represent certain lengths of time, three hundred and ninety days for Israel lying on his left side, forty days for Jerusalem lying on his right side. He is to proclaim that the number of days represents the number of years before the judgment of Israel and Jerusalem. He is to proclaim that the number of the days of his dreadful experience represents the number of years that Israel and Jerusalem will suffer.

The principle that interprets the time element in the prophecy is stated in Ezekiel 4:5, 6: 'I assign you a day for a year'.

This is now taken by the emerging Advent group, and is extended, to mean that whenever the term 'day' occurs in a prophetic, i.e. an apocalyptic context, it represents a literal year of three hundred and sixty days. The passage is now elevated into a principle. It will be applied beyond its original context to apocalyptic passages in both Old and New Testaments.

The grand speculation accepted for the Millerite interpretation is then taken as the code-breaking key to any and all predictions expressed in Scripture in such temporal terms. To this is added the principle that the selected terms 'time' or 'year' (representing three hundred and sixty days) means the corresponding number of literal years. This is exemplified in Hiram's Edson's hermeneutic.

Steps in the argument

The passage being interpreted is *Daniel* 8:14: 'Unto two thousand three hundred days, then shall the sanctuary be cleansed.' These are the steps taken:

1 A prophetic 'day' means a literal year.

2 A prophetic 'time' means a prophetic year and that means three hundred and sixty literal years

3 Two separate prophetic passages are coordinated: *Daniel* 9 and *Daniel* 8

4 The starting point of one is assumed to be the starting point of the other.

What was now needed was a starting point to get the application going. This was found in the date of the commandment for the restoration and rebuilding of Jerusalem (cf. the pronouncement of *Daniel* 9:25. This date, BCE 457 was taken to apply both to the

Seventh-day Adventists Interpreting Scripture

prophecy of chapter 8 and to the prophecies of chapter 9. In the former case it led eventually to a specific date of AD. 1844.

5 A speculation is now added about the sanctuary that is in heaven.

6 Passages in the book of Revelation are to be attached to the 1844 interpretation by means of claims about the heavenly sanctuary.

7 A thousand year period ends with execution of the final divine judgment.

Leroy E. Froom made a grand attempt to defend and to justify the hermeneutic in his series, *The Prophetic Faith of Our Fathers*. This is not the place to discuss the criticisms of his attempt to defend the method. Suffice it to say that reviews commended the comprehensive range of the research, but questioned the limited prophetic hermeneutic it set out to defend, thus rejecting the value of the enterprise as a successful apologetic for the Adventist prophetic interpretation.

011 'VISIONS' TAKEN AS AUTHORITATIVE

The claim to visionary experiences was welcomed at the time of the Disappointment and continued later. It became a widespread, common feature of various communities that claims to divine authority were made for such 'visions'. The reason was that when the claim to having had a visionary experience was accepted as a divine communication of some kind, the phenomenon was interpreted to endorse the teaching to which it was related. It is an example of the belief that unusual phenomena might reasonably be interpreted as having a divine source, and so a confirmatory function of the teaching to which they related. It was relatively easy to claim to have a vision. It is quite another matter to claim divine and confirmatory authority for that visionary experience, or for the ideas it was claimed to represent and endorse. It was a very serious step that a community took to accept the 'seer' as a continuing presence and a serious authority, as the manifestation of the divine even if was not an unusual phenomenon

Moreover, it was not unusual for an insight or idea (without a vision) to be called a vision. That is still an acceptable usage of the term. The phrase 'Do you see?' means 'Do you get the idea?' Because of that acceptable usage of 'vision' as idea, concept or insight, the ideas were readily called 'visions' and, once made, the claims were easily believed to point to some kind of visual experience. Indeed, calling an insight a 'vision' regularly expressed endorsement or approval of the idea or concept. It was often taken to set it apart as having special significance. It was not simply a kind of heavy underlining but taken a step further. What the 'seer' saw was taken as divine communication, and thus as divine endorsement of the position being discussed.

Take one use of the term 'see'. 'Do you see what I mean?' is not asking whether you have had a visual experience, but just whether you have got the point. So the answer 'I see what you mean' says, 'I have got the point.' It does not suggest that I have had a visual experience. The listener does not have to believe that the speaker has had a visual experience. But there is no escaping an expressed claim to vision. Its status is open to examination. But given this usage the hearer does not have to assume a particular visual phenomenon as source of the seeing, or insight.

Do you see what I am saying?

An interesting fact of word usage in English is that 'seer' is used as a synonym for 'prophet'.

An interesting question emerges. Take the case of a vision in which there appears a figure, preferably a heavenly or unusual one, who speaks or acts. What is the significance of the words and actions within the context of the vision, and the context in real life of the community or believer to whom the visionary communicates it? If the prophet, the 'seer', interprets the vision as endorsing doctrinal or ethical claims, even giving divine authority to them, under what circumstances is the community justified in adopting that interpretation?

Because of an assumption of divine guidance, the vision could be and was given a special status and authority. So 'visions' could influence the framers of doctrine and framers of doctrine could influence 'visions'. So a person who says 'I saw that . . . .' may be taken to mean more than, 'I had an idea'. The visionary may indeed claim, 'I had a visual experience and that gives special weight to what I am claiming, which claim you will recognise!

Does this mean that only when there is a visual experience or, which may be different, a claim to a visual experience, that the claim that follows its recital is divinely inspired? What shall we say of claims, directions and proposals made by the 'seer' when there has been no accompanying vision? To what extent may the license to claim a divine inspired source be extended, if at all when no such seeing has occurred? In any case, the hearer must assess the seer's report of the experience if, as is often the case, he receives it at second hand?

Let us imagine that, as is the case with any instance of interpretation, there is often a predisposition to interpret the vision or series of visions in a particular way. Since the vision has to be interpreted, the receivers of the vision, sometimes called 'prophets' and their audience must interpret the meaning of the vision and assess how words spoken and how actions performed in it are to be interpreted, what status they are to have. The status of the 'seer' is assessed positively when the vision is accepted as authentic, and the interpretation of the vision deemed to be the right one. *Indeed, the interpretation may be as important as the content of the 'seeing.'* As with any case of interpretation, the particular understanding of the content of the vision will demand discernment, explanation and defence, as will indeed the process employed in the making of the particular interpretation. Here, both the present as well as the original context is all important in assessing that content.

The term 'prophet' for most of us means a person who predicts the future. The scriptural meaning of the term is different. It means simply 'one who speaks for another', especially one who speaks for God. What the prophet says may refer to the present or to the future, or be simply some kind of admonition, warning or reproof. Sometimes its source is in a vision something 'seen' by the prophet. Hence he is also called a 'seer'. That term is neutral as regards present or future application of the vision.

012 SHIFT OF EMPHASIS

In the 1844 context, the emphasis was on prediction. The word 'prophet' then had the narrower significance. This continued after the Disappointment. The concern of the developing Advent Movement (the group of Adventists who later were to insist on the obligation to keep holy the seventh day Sabbath) was not only with what God was going to do in relation to the world, but what was going to be their future as an emerging community. Hence the importance (in late 1844) of the shift of emphasis from the destruction of world as cosmos to divine activity in the heavens and what would follow it. Since that heavenly activity in the sanctuary was to continue, no-one knew for how long, there was a future of the emerging Advent community. The earlier concern was with apocalyptic writings. These were taken as on a par with other kinds of writing, indeed given priority for the purposes of interpretation. But as we have seen, a distinctive hermeneutic was produced to interpret these distinctive writings.

They were to be taken literally, in the sense of 'referring to real events in the world in the future', a kind of telling history in reverse. All will happen in God's good time. But such knowledge is revealed only to those who had the correct code to decipher the hidden meaning of the symbolic passages. This claim was a common feature of apocalyptic writings from other cultures. It was not unique to the Old and New Testaments.

Since they consisted in statements about lengths of time, the effort was rewarded when other statements about time were discovered in Scripture, and used to provide the desired clue. As we have seen (cf. paragraph 23), the term 'day' was taken to mean a 'year' of 360 days. This was derived from a selected passage from the book of *Ezekiel*. The term 'day' there represents a literal year. Ezekiel is instructed to perform certain acts for a given number of days. These acts represent what is to happen to Judah and Israel in the same number of years. What that means is not further considered. The principle is isolated from its context and becomes the clue to interpret the 'days' of the passage in *Daniel*.

Then there is the term 'time' as in the expression, 'time, times and the dividing of time' (K. J. V.) , more accurately rendered as 'a time, two times and half a time'. (RSV). *Daniel* 12:7; *Revelation* 12;14 'Time' means 'year', and since 'year' consisted of 360 days, so within a prophetic passage 'time' means 360 literal years. So the complete phrase points to a period of 1,260 literal years. Find a starting point and you can get an ending point. From A.D. 538 brings us to 1798, identified by the Advent interpreters as the beginning of the 'time of the end'.

Note: AD 538 marks the downfall of imperial Rome at the hand of the Ostrogoths and the beginning of the power of the Papacy. In 1798 Berthier, for the French government, took the pope prisoner in Rome and so ended the political rule of the Papacy.

013 CONVICTIONS CONFIRMED (JAMES AND ELLEN WHITE)

The focus has now moved from earth to the heavenly spheres, where judgment is going on. Now that the year 1844 had become established, it was held that a process of judgment was to be connected with operations in the heavenly sanctuary. Thus Adventist interpreters were attracted to a passage in the book of Revelation, 'The hour of his judgment has come'. This is the first of three angels' messages, and has come to be a key passage, setting the commandment keepers against 'Babylon', 'the beast and its image'. *Revelation* 14:6-12.

Adventist interpreters, concerned with memories of the medieval papacy, had identified the papal system with the 'beast', and this they now carried over into the understanding of this passage. The result was that so-called 'apostate Protestantism' was now identified as included in the expression, 'those that worship the beast and its image'. The basis for this was their refusal to accept the demands being made by the 'remnant'. These were that they keep all the commandments (as the text indicates) including in particular, the reverencing of the Sabbath.

Discussion among Adventists led to the introduction of a third entity, namely spiritualism. They predicted a 'threefold union' as the great persecuting power before the final manifestation of God's wrath against the persecutors. The Scripture described that last judgment in horrible detail: 'fire and brimstone in presence of the holy angels and in the presence of the Lamb . . . the smoke of their torment goes up for ever and ever'. . . . 'and blood flowed from the winepress' vv. 10-11, 20.

These teachings were accepted and endorsed and remain as doctrine. Indeed the 'three angels messages' became a definition of Adventist doctrine. Pictorial depictions of three angels in flight in mid heaven are to be frequently seen in literature and in church buildings. These symbols provide believers with a reminder of how important these teachings are.

Another pillar of Adventism derives from an interpretation of *Revelation* 19:10. The angel, whose self-description is 'a fellow servant with you and your brethren who hold the testimony of Jesus', in a description of the believing community, says, 'For the testimony of Jesus is the spirit of prophecy'. This is intended as a feature of the whole congregation of believers. The community has 'the prophetic spirit' (a better translation), and that consists in its testimony to Jesus. It describes the whole congregation of Christians as a community of witness to Jesus Christ. That defines its mission. However, Adventists identify the meaning of the passage in a much more restricted way.

It was quite common in groups in mid-nineteenth century Eastern America that some believers, both men and women, laid claim to visions and other unusual phenomena. It was a means of getting attention to and getting authority for what they had to say. It often led to fanaticism.

The Advent Movement had among them a woman who claimed to have visions linking her directly with angel messengers and to the mediated immediacy of God. The Adventist community accepted this interpretation of the unusual phenomena she manifested, and took her speaking and writings as direct messages mediated from a divine source. She was given a unique status in the community that has been maintained to the present time. She is recognised as a prophet, and her writings are called 'the spirit of prophecy'. So it is accepted that when one hears, 'The spirit of prophecy says. . . .' and a passage from her writing is quoted, it is to be taken as authoritative. Often a quotation from her writing is prefaced with the words. 'Inspiration says . . . .' The intention is the same, namely to set her words apart as 'canonical'. Take notice, for these words have a special status! It relies on the questionable assumption that the idea of 'inspiration' is unambiguous, appropriate, and confirming.

What is certain is that, within the church, her writings are circulated, read and quoted as no other writings are. For many Adventists a reference to E. G. White, under the form 'Inspiration says. . . .' typically but questionably means that the matter is settled, put beyond question, that her interpretations of biblical texts are to be accepted as making other interpretations unnecessary. That is rather frustrating for teachers of the New Testament who have mastery of the Greek language and for teachers of the Old Testament who have mastery of Hebrew. It is part of a widespread but mistaken conviction within the church that the writings of E G W set limits to our understanding of Scripture.

One interesting observation is relevant here. Ellen Gould White frequently listened to discussions and debates. She admitted that she did not always understand. Frequently, she endorsed some results of such discussion and that endorsement gave authority to those teachings in preference to others. What is certain is that the teachings that she endorsed gave her new material for her visions. Later visions reflected earlier discussion, endorsing one view over another. She was often a mouth-piece rather than an originator. She was, as 'prophet' characteristically reflective. Some apologists for her authority have stressed this facet, by laying emphasis on the divine origin and communication of the pronouncements. They have often employed the notion of inspiration for this purpose, without adequately considering the meaning of this often misunderstood concept. Her 'seeing' was often reflective of what she had recently heard.

From time to time she would make predictions. Some of these failed. She wholeheartedly embraced the prophetic hermeneutic of her contemporaries, the inheritance from William Miller. The one prediction that connects with our preceding discussion is the following:

Through the two great errors, the immortality of the soul and Sunday sacredness, Satan will bring the people under his deceptions. While the former lays the foundation of Spiritualism, the latter creates a bond of sympathy with Rome. The Protestants of the United States will be foremost in stretching their hands across the gulf to grasp the hand of Spiritualism; they will reach over the abyss to clasp hands with the Roman power; and under the influence of this threefold union, this country will follow in the steps of Rome in trampling on the rights of conscience.[1]

The disappointed members of the post 1844 Advent movement were so confident of their positions that they were able to find passages of Scripture that they could interpret to correspond to

---

1   Ellen G. White, *The Great Controversy between Christ and Satan*. Pacific Press Publishing Association, 1911, p. 588.

the details of their recent experience. We have seen this in the case of the interpretation of the parable of the Virgins. There are other cases. To mention just one more: James White wrote, interpreting a passage from the book of Revelation taken as key, that their present situation corresponded to the content of the passage about the fall of Babylon. Upset that their insistence on the keeping of the Sabbath was not being accepted by many Adventist groups, James White applied the judgment of the second angel to these groups, 'Babylon is fallen' and so they are ripe for condemnation. Given the opportunity to endorse Sabbath keeping which the Advent Movement had seen as a divine obligation, James White and his contemporaries identified those groups who declined the invitation to keep the Sabbath as 'Babylon'. They made an immediate application of the text.

Later the words will be given a much wider application, in the quotation above, to American Protestantism, fallen because of its refusal to obey the commandments, and its liaison with Catholics and spiritualists. That is a prediction not fulfilled in over a century. But in its first application the interpretation served to confirm and strengthen the firmly held conviction of White and his group that their reading of Scripture and course of action were divinely guided. Their confidence was undiminished. They were speaking divine truth with unquestionable assurance. We might summarise their assurance as follows:

Our approach to and our resulting understanding of the Scriptures we have selected confirm our belief in specific divine guidance in our very recent history. We believe that the events of our experience correspond to Scriptural prophecy. That strengthens our confidence to go forward.

The conviction remained with the developed community that the inheritance from the post Disappointment days must remain unchanged. This was voiced in no uncertain tones by E. G. White. A typical expression is the following.

No line of our faith that has made us what we are is to be weakened. We have the old landmarks of truth, experience, and duty, and we are to stand firm in defence of our principles, in full view of the world.[2]

The claim is quite clear, even if it is expressed in vague terms. The reader is expected to know what the line and landmarks are, representing the conclusions reached after much debate by 'the pioneers'. Once agreed upon, we are told they are not to be further discussed but simply accepted. Then there was room for debate and discussion. Now the 'official' demand is for simple, unquestioning acceptance and propagation of their conclusions, based as they were on their way of approaching Scripture. There was never any question about the narrowly defined prophetic interpretation of Scripture that produced the conclusions now elevated to acceptable doctrine which the faithful are obliged to endorse.

Orthodoxy has become defined, and was thereafter demanded, as in the quotation above. Official attitudes that repeat the sentiment of the above quotation may harden even to the extent that they may be expressed uncompromisingly in such terms as follows.

We stand firmly behind the accepted teachings and consider any questionings as betrayal.

We shall not speak of progress to the new.

We shall speak rather of retention of the old, as

We insist on repeating the thoughts of the pioneers..

That, I find, stands in obvious contradiction to the demand made in the same writer's book, Education, where it states that the purpose of education is to train the youth to be 'thinkers and not mere reflectors of other men's thoughts' (p. 17). That is a worthy aim for the teacher. It has been my aim, and where I have been successful I have met with gratitude. Where I have not been successful it has been quite a different story.

---

2 'No Change in God's Cause'. *Testimony* Vol. 8. No 36.

014 REFLECT

If I had known what would happen or not happen, I would not have been so certain. My attitude would have been different. I would not have trusted my feeling of certainty. But I did not know the future, since it had not yet happened. It came out the way I did not expect. However, I should have considered other possible outcomes.

If she had known the future, she would not have said what on several occasions she said about the future. But we know a century and many decades later what she did not know. But we do not know what will be our future. We shall be wise not to make predictions.

II ADVENTIST HERMENEUTIC
Why is 'interpretation' such an important issue?

1. The dominant stress in S. D. A teaching is on the primary authority of the biblical text.

2. S. D. As. insist that equal authority is to be given to what results from interpreting the Bible. The doctrine, the 'message' has divine authority. It is also primary, the *raison d'être* of the organisation.

3 How you interpret the Scriptures in order to establish doctrine is thus a primary and crucial issue. Put it in the form of question: How do you get from the voluminous and varied content of Scripture to selective, distinctive and exclusive Adventist doctrine? The answer consists in holding the focus, in the case of the Adventist, to a restricted prophetic kind of interpretation. The reading of Scripture for the purpose of establishing doctrine is to be distinguished from other purposes of reading it, the devotional for example.

4. To take Scripture as source of doctrine, the question of inspiration is quite subsidiary to the question of interpretation.[3]

The point is that, however it got to you, you are dealing with the text, however it was transmitted and whatever you say about its status as a result. You start with the conviction of the authority of Scripture. You then develop doctrines by interpreting the chosen Scripture you take as authoritative. Those doctrines then, it is claimed, have the same authority that Scripture has.

Of course, Adventists give reasons for taking Scripture as authoritative. Along with other conservative Christians the appeal is

---

[3] For the discussion of the issue see my *Seventh-day Adventists and the Bible*, Nottingham: Evening Publication, 2004, and *From Inspiration to Understanding*, Gonzalez, Florida: Energion Publications, 2011.

made to the claim that the text is inspired. That is not the question we are here discussing. Suffice it to say that appeal to inspiration does not establish the authority claimed for Scripture.

Since Adventist doctrine is unique, and since Adventists are so firmly convinced that it is true doctrine and that only they have the truth and since also that they have the obligation of propagating it worldwide, the question of its derivation from Scripture is the crucial question. How did they get this result? The issue of the interpretation of Scripture is not only an issue. It is the issue.

Seventh day Adventists exist today because they accept and continue to reapply the method of interpretation of William Miller for their crucial and distinctive doctrinal appeal. He described his employment of Scripture as concordance dependent and 'promiscuous'.

A problem with the content of that (prophetic) interpretation must focus on two items: first, the fact that the Advent, repeatedly claimed over many decades to be about to happen immediately has not happened, so the 'signs' once said to indicate the imminence now have become irrelevant.

And second, the grand prediction of widespread persecution of the faithful, has not taken place. This is a new departure. The crucial example is from Revelation 14, the phrase, 'Babylon is fallen'. This judgment was applied by Adventists first to those contemporaries following 1844 who did not accept the obligation to keep the Seventh day as the Sabbath as the Adventists presented it, and later to the whole of the Protestant establishment, said to be 'fallen'. That was a very bold move! Whatever else they claim or do, and that is a very great deal, this way of interpreting remains primary and is taken for granted, giving the church its self-reference, and producing its ecclesiastical introversiveness that then is projected outside. The interpretative method grounds the community's conviction of plausible, indeed indubitable, certainty. It provides for some pride in being exclusive, and in being divinely appointed to an exclusive responsibility.

This led to self-reference. 'We are the ones who are fulfilling the prophetic description of the text. For, we are the ones who are "keeping the commandments." Moreover, we have the testimony of Jesus which is the "spirit of prophecy". This term is given a restrictive application to a prophetic voice of one individual within the community, rather than being taken as having reference to the whole community as having the 'prophetic spirit' (a better translation). This restrictive interpretation of the apocalyptic passage enables the Adventists to say, 'It is we who are the people of prophecy, the divinely appointed voice of God for the last days. It is our task to warn the whole world of God as Judge and of the final judgment, while we set the example in keeping the commandments. We are the bearers of the final message to mankind. We provide the last opportunity to hear the truth.' So alternatives are relativized. There has been a great narrowing.

Once the framework of the Adventist prophetic interpretation had become firmly established, later contexts provided occasions for the application of the principle to other non-prophetic passages of Scripture, for example the parables, e. g. of the virgins, and for the crucial rendering of the three angels' messages of Revelation 14. It is to be noted that these interpretations are rooted in and applied directly to the Adventists' disappointment experiences. This is a new departure. The principle is: We interpret our experience by applying the selected text directly to that experience, because we see it directly relevant to, indeed we find a direct fit, with our own experience. Since it so directly fits, we take it as our assurance of providential prophetic guidance. It is as if the text was written just for us!

How shall we proceed? Let us take the ideas of revival and of reformation for guidance. To revive means 'to bring back'. To reform means 'to effect a good change.' Revival happens to the past. The idea in general is (somehow) to bring back the past, especially if one thinks that something valuable has been lost. Reformation happens in and to the present. The idea here is to produce something more acceptable than what already exists or has persisted.

We are our history and our inheritance, depending on what we do with that heritage. We may do little or nothing to change it, but simply try to keep it as intact as we can.

Features of the Restrictive Hermeneutic

First, the focus is restricted. The interest is in detailed prediction. That is not the theme of most of Scripture.

Second, the interest is in numerical interpretation of the figures in the chosen text.

Third, the sources are largely restricted to apocalyptic passages and those that were thought to be immediately connected with such passages.

Fourth, each of these is considered without due consideration of their immediate context, but as contributing to the development of prophecy, and clarifying the experience of the expectant community.

Fifth, the method is then to find situations and phenomena in the real world, in history, for the application of the predictions. Where lengths of time are specified in the text this involved finding applications for these.

Sixth, and crucial, is the year-day principle. Wherever 'day' is used in the text it means a literal 360 day year. Where 'time' is used it also means a literal 360 day year.

Seventh, to unravel 2,300 days (= years) of *Daniel* 8:14, the dominating, crucial text, a starting point is needed. The procedure was to connect one time span with another. Connect the predictions in *Daniel* 8:14, (two thousand three hundred days) with those *Daniel* 9, (seventy weeks) using the day for a year principle and then assume the same starting point for both. Then find an event at the end of the period worked out that fits and take that as fulfillment.

What gets overlooked in this procedure

1. A serious consideration of the general features of apocalyptic and its intended function in the Hebrew communities who have suffered and are suffering threat, persecution, death and destruction.

2. What also gets neglected is a serious consideration of what is involved in a balanced and reasonable approach to the whole of Scripture. For the Christian this means attention as priority to what Luther called the Christ-principle: All Scripture is to be interpreted by reference to Jesus Christ. If we reapply older texts to a different context, we have to justify that juxtapositioning.

3. The radical shift of focus and emphasis in designating the idea of 'sanctuary'. In its original context it refers to the essential centre of Hebrew worship. This was the Temple, where an elaborate series of regulated activities was carried out. This involved a careful distinction between priest and sacrifice. Adventists ignored both of these things.

The idea of 'cleansing' now does not mean the renewal of worship in a restored centre of worship after its physical destruction. It means a process of mediation by Christ as the God-man, bridging the gap between sinful man and just God.

Moreover, what is also assumed now is a Christian context as the appropriate reference. That is a very bold move, made by Miller himself and endorsed by Adventists. For him the 'sanctuary' was the earth. This was revised by Edson and became standard teaching by Adventists. The sanctuary is a location in 'heaven'. A radical change has taken place from Miller. The problematical reference is that 1844 seems to mark a beginning. Or, does it? At any rate for Adventists in later 1844 it now marks a beginning and not an end. The end becomes unknown, somewhere in the future, but by no means specifiable. What is certain is no one knows when the end will be. It is also a conjecture as to what is actually going on in this sanctuary in heaven. Here it is assumed the priest and the sacrifice are one. So all kinds of complications emerge with this revised concept of 'sanctuary', taken as it is out of its Hebrew context. What has 1844 to do with the baroque symbolism of the book of *Hebrews*?

A radical revision of the meaning of 'sanctuary' and of 'cleansing' has taken place. For the new Adventist interpretation, a Christian context, and a rather particular one, is created and then assumed as the appropriate reference. That of course was assumed in Miller's bold move. Assuming that Christian context, the radical revision is made by Hiram Edson and followed in the emerging community, that the 'sanctuary' is located in heaven, where a quite different function and set of activities is taking place. The 1844 date now marks a beginning not an end, as with Miller. The book of *Hebrews* had suggested it at the end of the first century. Is this the beginning of the heavenly process of mediation? What is certain is that the new concept of the heavenly sanctuary marked a real beginning for the emerging Adventist community. But no-one knows when the end will be, when the process of heavenly mediation will end. It does not follow that to recognise a heavenly sanctuary at a point in time that the activity said to be taking place within it began at that point of recognition. What did begin then was a renewal of hope for renewal of hope and for continuing belief. That was a decisive stage in the history of the Advent movement, made possible by an acceptance of the proposed speculation what me might call, call it 'Edson's hypothesis' or 'Edson's speculation' .

All kinds of complications now newly emerge. Discovered in 1844, how is such mediation connected with the ascension? Is the new interpretation saying that the mediation is literally taking place somewhere in the immensities of space, or is it rather a symbolic way of representing the idea of atonement. One notes that the concept of atonement as mediation assumes a kind of Anselmian background.

In his work, *Cur Deus Homo* (Why God Man?), Anselm develops the idea of the person of the God-man, who only can bridge the gap between God and man since he alone partakes of both divine and human natures.

So we might ask, 'What connection does the baroque observations and constructions of the book of *Hebrews* have with this Adventist teaching? For Adventists, the belief is that the sanctuary is literal, somewhere within the heavens and Jesus the Mediator, who is also the sacrifice, is located and active therein. We know that the universe is extensive beyond all imagination. Some suggestion as to what such literalism means must be forthcoming. Otherwise we must be puzzled and simply take the elaborate scheme as a suggestive pictorial aid to understanding. That seems hard to do for the Adventist interpreter.

The S. D. A. church is a complicated community. It has many departments. Each of these demands very different skills and competences, to mention a few: medical, business, administrative, organisational, mechanical, educational. Each of these demands a variety of skills as they are themselves divided into contrasting groups of labour. Most of them demand different and contrasting sorts of professional knowledge and competence. The skills demanded in one department may not often overlap with those of another. One would not expect the business man to make the judgments regarding a patient's medical treatment that were in the sphere of the doctor's professional knowledge. One would not expect a business expert to make judgments that a professional theologian would be able to make. Different competences working in unity make for efficient levels of cooperation.

Now Seventh- day Adventism is a religious organisation. That means it has a history. But the exercise of these specialised competences does not require knowledge of the history that has produced the organisation, nor indeed of the doctrines that characterise its uniqueness. Specialised decisions are regularly made with quite secular knowledge.

But there is another overall context in which, as a church, all these competences are exercised. Within that context you can be an excellent, specialised physician, and have little professional competence about education. So to maintain unity each member of the community must have something essential in common. The question we must ask is: What is that something that we must share to be and remain a particular religious community?'

It can be answered in various ways. There are two basic answers that unfortunately are sometimes confused.

1 To be a united community we must share Christian faith.

2 To be a united community we must share doctrine and share it in some detail. That involves conforming to a set of specified beliefs

3 To be an Adventist community we must share both Christian faith and also share the doctrine as established within the church, by partaking in the results of our early history.

4 To be an Adventist community means doing good in the world, incidentally, continuously, professionally, in cooperation with any and all good people like-minded to do good.

So there is occasion for tension, between being critically exclusive and having our overwhelming concern to promote doctrine and in joining activities with those whose Christian faith we share but differ in doctrine and also with those without Christian faith. It would not be entirely and always appropriate to voice the remnants and developments of Millerite apocalypticism when we are cooperating with others in saving life, bringing relief and comfort to those in abject distress, planning ahead and engaging in common activity may not need the making specific identification of beliefs.

Reflect

If I had known what would happen or not happen, I would not have been so certain. My attitude would have been different. But I did not know the future, since it had not yet happened. It came out the way I did not expect. However, I should have considered other possible outcomes.

If she had known the future she would not have said what on several occasions she said about the future. But we know a century and many decades later that she did not know. But we do not know what will be our future.

While Adventists recognise the divine authority of the Biblical text, there is a crucial observation that must be recognised. In interpreting the significance of the Hebrew tabernacle/sanctuary it is the following guiding and important assumption. A crucial purpose of the earthly sanctuary service was to reveal – in symbols, in types, in minor-prophecies – the death and high priestly ministry of Jesus.

That is the principle that, when applied as Adventists apply it, renders a very complex account by examining and applying the details of the Hebrew sanctuary services. It is the one guiding hermeneutical principle with regard to the Levitical system of sacrifices and rituals that the Adventists have seen as essential. That happened only after the assumption that the 'sanctuary' is in heaven where the ascended Christ is now ministering, proposed by Hiram Edson in 1844 after the Disappointment.

That assumption served the immediate purpose of reassuring the Adventists that all was not lost. It assured them that time would stretch out for longer. But there was no suggestion as to how long the continuing time would be. So Adventists were content to use the term 'soon' and then qualified it radically by saying: 'We do not know how soon', in other words, 'we do not know what we mean by 'soon'. But beyond that immediate function of providing assurance, it led to a multitude of speculations, when propositions about the activity of Christ as priest/high priest were primarily drawn initially from details of the Hebrew sanctuary and its services. These were now given prominence, even primary significance, in the process of interpreting Scripture. It dominates the hermeneutic as selected details of the sanctuary service are transposed and transformed into a Christian and post-Disappointment context.

11 How to Understand an Adventist

Here is a form of life. This is what they do. This is how they speak. This is the way they use language. This language is used. You don't have to accept it to understand. You have to see how it is used. To understand Adventists you have to realise the seriousness with which they take the following positions.

1. **The Bible has authority.** The Bible is like a bag of building blocks. The principle is that you pick from its pages 'here a little, there a little.' You set 'line upon line.' until a doctrine is built. Adventists justify this approach by pointing to the prophetic and doctrinal system which they have constructed by using the method.

2. **Expectation of the Second Advent.** Adventists, they claim, are a people of prophecy. They are a community that fulfills prophecy. Their voice is the 'Voice of Prophecy'. This ties them with the early Adventists of the mid-nineteenth century. They are commended for their fervent hoping and Adventists try to maintain the fervour of their hope. Such is difficult to sustain in view of the passage of time and the not taking place of the Advent. Some Adventists are uneasy.

3. **Belief in possession of *the truth*.** Adventists use such terms as 'being in the truth' for a good Adventist, 'going out of the truth' for someone who has stopped being an Adventist. You often hear the claim, 'We have the truth.' The truth refers to the body of teachings which constitutes the doctrine of the church. The two basic truths are the Sabbath and the soon coming of Jesus. But these are accompanied by a very complex system, springing from the idea of the 'sanctuary'. Adventists insist that the truth is simple. But often they do not realise how complicated their system is.

4. **Acceptance of the writings of Ellen White as the voice of God in the church.** The collecting, arranging and indexing of the corpus of her writings has been a preoccupation. You cannot understand Adventists without realising that in practice they give her writings primacy over all others. It is often the case that more attention is given to the repetition of Ellen White's writing than to serious textual and contextual study of the Scriptures. The author of a typical book is far more concerned to repeat White than to understand what the synoptic Gospels teach about the Kingdom of God and about Jesus' understanding of his mission, even when the topic of the book is the Second Advent. In this book you get the Bible through the views of White. That is quite the norm in Adventist literature and lesson books. An oft repeated slogan expresses this attitude: These writings constitute 'a lesser light to illuminate the greater light' of Scripture. How are we to understand this duet of metaphors? For many Adventists it means that what the writings say in interpreting Scripture is the definitive word. Her interpretation sets a boundary for understanding, interpreting the particular words of Scripture.

5. **Ecclesiastical introversiveness.** Adventists feel a self-sufficiency within their community. This shows itself in many ways. I mention two: the not reading of literature which is not of Adventist origin and the discouragement of educational contact outside the community. Children must go to Adventist schools. This is coupled with an anti-theological, anti-philosophical bias. An Adventist is likely to read a book published outside of the Adventist circle only if it is about Adventists, only likely to read a theological article if it makes reference to Adventist teaching. Moreover an Adventist author is likely to get his book with doctrinal content published, only if there is a direct and obvious connection with Adventist teaching, and also if it is written with due simplicity.

6. **A non-contextual approach to Scripture,** which (1) leads to an indifference to context, to original problems and to worldviews. (2) It sometimes leads, as is inevitable, to a grand indifference

to the wider meaning of and in the passage, of for example the parable, and the world view. You get what you want but you miss the vision or the beauty. Let me illustrate. Here, and you may find it hard to believe, one writer is arguing that the Bible is reliable because the Bible writers made correct statements about the cosmos. The prophet believed that the earth was spherical. Isaiah said that God sits on the circle of the earth.[4]

Overlooking that 'sits' is metaphorical (so why is not 'circle' too?) the writer misses entirely the grand vision of the sovereignty of God so beautifully portrayed in the passage. Another example of such special pleading (which we discuss later) is the interpretation of 'my Lord delayeth his coming' in the parable. 'Delay' doesn't mean that the master has postponed his arrival (or departure) It means that the wicked servant has a subjective apprehension. The delay is subjective, in the mind of the wicked servant. There is no real delay. The writer has no time, in pursuing his point (which is to say that God has not delayed the Second Coming, even if Adventists have often and reasonably thought so) to ask for the significance of the parable and its relevance for Jesus' teaching about the kingdom of God. But that was not our author's concern anyway. His primary concern is not Jesus' teaching but Ellen White's.

7. **Adventists are the remnant.** They are the people of prophecy. Since the biblical prophecies point to the present time as the end time (more on this later), since the Adventists come into being as a direct result of acknowledging the prophecies, and since they were predicted in Scripture, they are God's special people. So there is a sense of security. This attitude is sometimes somewhat disturbed by those worthies who insist that it is faith not works that is essential.

8. **Without some understanding of AD 1844, there is no understanding of Adventists.** So we must ask the question, how do we get to 1844 and what follows? It will take a little effort to explain this. It is clear that AD 1844 is a crucial date. The method

---

4   'Adventist Review', 3 March 1994, 10. The passage in question is *Isaiah* 40:22 'sitteth on the circle of the earth'

by which we arrive at it is not simple. In fact it is very complex. To understand how we get at the date, I shall first state the assumptions which have to be made and after that the procedures that must be taken.[5]

ASSUMPTIONS

1 The general assumption is of the building block approach to Scripture. One picks here and there and puts the selections together to 'prove' the biblical doctrine.

2 *Daniel* refers to events far in the future, writing far in advance of the events he mentions.[6]

---

[5] After the Disappointment the believers had to make a decision. Should they admit the error of the dating ,or should they admit the error of the hermeneutic? The early Adventists decided to retain Miller's method of interpretation and the date, 1844, it had produced. But, while doing so find and endorse a new application for the key text by reinterpreting the reference of the key term in the text, namely 'the sanctuary'. For this a bold speculation was needed. Hiram Edson supplied it. . He proposed a radical change of focus in the application of the method. Look to heaven and not to the immediate destruction of the earth. The sanctuary is in heaven.

[6] The assumption made by Adventists is that Daniel is not contemporary with the events he portrays, i.e. he was not contemporary with Antiochus IV. The corollary is that Daniel's visions do not refer to the course of events being played out in Israel and that he did not really understand what he was seeing in vision and what he was writing. That this is an assumption can be readily seen when we consider the alternative, which consists of its denial. That is to say, Daniel was contemporary with events which he represents in the symbols and figures and dates he uses. By using symbols he can vividly portray the message of courage and hope to his harassed and courageous countrymen who are fighting and giving their lives to preserve their faith and the faith of their people. That message was that the Kingdom of God was about to come. The present struggles of the Maccabeus against their rulers are to be the ultimate part of history before the breaking in of the visible Kingdom of God on earth. The situation of the people, persecuted, harassed, keeping faith and high in expectation, is the paradigm for all the apocalyptic messages which would come later. Interpreted in this way, Daniel bears a striking

3 Puzzling apocalyptic passages require a key so we can understand them. One day in the text stands for a year in real time. (The notable exception is the thousand years of *Revelation*).

4 The two time periods, the seventy weeks (interpreted in terms of 70 x 7 days) and the two thousand three hundred days, must be connected as Daniel's intention and so in interpreting him.

5 Both periods must have the same starting point.

6 Jesus can be introduced into the very fabric of the prophecy.

7 We can move from the Hebrew context, from a reference to the Old Testament sanctuary in *Daniel* via the book of *Hebrews* to speak of Jesus as High Priest and to expound a procedure for this sanctuary in heaven. We can work this out in great detail.

8 Reject, as the primary meaning of *Daniel*, the notion of a literal cleansing the Hebrew temple, which had been defiled by earthly conquerors, destroyed in fact.

9 The heavenly sanctuary is literally 'in the heavens'.

10 One year in the Hebrew sanctuary ritual is a symbol of the whole course of events in the heavenly sanctuary.

11 Our time registers in the events that take place there. A point in time here (AD 1844) has its counterpart there. This rests on the further assumptions:

12 Jesus is now in a space-time which is both like ours and in some sense continuous with ours, which entails:

13 Jesus is a physical being.

---

resemblance to the message and envisaged situation of the Adventist in their hope and anticipation of struggle, persecution and death before the breaking in of the Kingdom. Interpreted in this way, it would appear that *Daniel* is rather more relevant to the Adventists' situation now than on the assumptions presented in the above text. It is worth considering.

Accounts of the events in Judah and Israel under Antiochus are readily available

We have listed the assumptions which are needed to get the procedure working. Adventists will probably be surprised if you call these 'assumptions' and if you insist that they need defence, that they need to be justified. That is because they take them so much for granted, and perhaps assume that they have already been justified. That does not alter the fact that they are assumptions and that they need in some cases explanation, in all cases justification. That means seriously considering alternatives.

PROCEDURES

1 Read the prediction about the seventy weeks: 70 weeks are to pass before Messiah appears (*Daniel* 7:24).

2 The days of these weeks are actually years: so 490 days is equal to 490 years.

3 The starting date is 457 BC, when a decree to rebuild the ruined Jerusalem was granted (*Daniel* 7:25).

4 Select the statement that it would be 2300 days before the defiled sanctuary would be restored (*Daniel* 8:13-14).

5 Connect this statement with the prophecy of 70 weeks.

6 Calculate from 457 BC, 2300 years. You get AD 1843.

7 So a period from AD 1843 to 1844 is indicated as the limit of the time of fulfillment

8 Do not interpret the sanctuary in the literal sense of the temple in Jerusalem

9 The sanctuary is in heaven

10 Jesus is to be introduced into the book of *Daniel*

11 Jesus is High Priest in the sanctuary

12 Interpret the Old Testament Day of Atonement (*Leviticus* 16) as a day of Judgment

13 Interpret the Day of Atonement as a process of 'cleansing' (*Leviticus* 16:29-34).

14 Transfer the notion of judgment and of 'cleansing' to Jesus in his sanctuary.

15 Conclude that AD 1844 marks the beginning of the Last Judgment.

16 Human opportunity for salvation comes to an end when the heavenly Day of Atonement ends. This is the 'end,' or 'close' of 'probation'.

17 Jesus then comes from the sanctuary to earth to execute judgment on the wicked. This has some parallel to the banishment of the scapegoat on the Hebrew Day of Atonement (*Leviticus* 16:20-22).

IV Back to the Gospels

The gospels may speak again and again.

It is because there is a direct parallel between the experience of the early church and the late twenty-first century experience of the Adventist church (and indeed of any Christian who has expected the advent to take place in their experience in the twentieth century). that the message of the gospels is now very relevant.

The message of the gospels is the message of Jesus. It is also the message about Jesus. For, at the resurrection the proclaimer became the proclaimed.

Jesus' message had already spoken to another situation of disappointment after the death of Jesus, a general disappointment among his disciples. Then they remembered his sayings and the revelation restored their confidence. Jesus' words were the occasion of god's revelation. Their hearts burned within them as he spoke to them, and then came the moment of revelation (cf. *Luke* 24).

To understand the message, you have to understand the context. There were several contexts to the message of Jesus.

Jesus spoke Aramaic in a Jewish context. His compatriots expected the setting up of the kingdom of god, which for them had to do with the nation. Their aspirations were nationalistic. Jesus spoke to them directly. But he also spoke to his disciples, sometimes explaining the inner meaning of his sayings.

Luke wrote Greek in a Christian context. It was also a context of expectation. His readers expected the Second Advent and they expected it soon. What is true of *Luke* is also true of the other gospels.

You and I read the gospels in English (or some other modern language) in the twentieth century.

It is important to think about this. Jesus spoke in one language. His words were reported in a different language. We read them in yet another language. But the difference in context is as important as the difference in language. Jesus spoke originally to Jews. The gospels are directed to Christians living in an ancient world. So the words of Jesus have different settings. That means that they will be given an interpretation that fits the setting.

When the Gospel writers produced the Gospels they had in mind the early Christian believers who were coming to terms with the realisation that the advent had not and would not take place quickly. They realised that the teaching of Jesus was most appropriate for this situation. They saw that Jesus' teaching about the Son of Man, and about the Kingdom of God was just what the early church needed. They realised that his setting some of this teaching in the form of striking and imaginative parables meant that the stories could live again and again in their different situation.

They may be so adapted to the new situation that it is as if they were spoken directly to that situation. The same words in a different situation may become part of the new situation, speak directly to it.

The historical question, a very fascinating one, is this: what did Jesus actually say? What are the actual words of Jesus? Given that we have Greek Gospels, how do we get from the context in which they were written, that of the church, now widely spread among the gentile territory, and at least thirty, and more likely fifty or sixty years after the death of Jesus, back to the actual sayings of Jesus. Remember Jesus spoke a different language than that of the gospels. So we can ask two kinds of question, What did the early church teach and believe? and What did Jesus teach and believe? What Jesus taught was taken and placed within the setting of the situation of the early church. The situation of the church as a whole was that by mid-century Jesus had not come back. The *parousia* had not taken place. The believers in this situation found in Jesus' teaching a message directly suited to their need. Those parables which were originally addressed to Jesus' opponents or to the crowds have now been applied by the early church to the Christian community. An earlier and seminal book on the parables observes that this led to an increasing shift of emphasis to the hortatory aspect, especially from the eschatological to the hortatory. What this means is that instead of urging the disciples that the advent was very, very soon, they shifted the emphasis and urged that in view of the advent, whenever it might be, they should be ready, do the right thing, be about the work of the church and the work of the world with joy. The author then adds, 'the primitive church related the parables to its own actual situation, whose chief features were the missionary motive and the delay of the *parousia*; it interpreted and expanded them with these factors in view.'

So if we now turn to the failure of the Adventist hope in the twentieth century we shall find that the gospels have the right message to offer, if it be heard.

The next step is to go to the gospels and take a sample of the teaching we find there, and show how very relevant it is to the situation in view, the new context of disappointment at the not taking place of the advent.

There is a wealth of material here, but since our purpose is simply to illustrate it will be sufficient to refer to some parables.

There are several parables which begin with the words, 'the kingdom of heaven is like. . . .'; then comes the comparison. It's like a grain of mustard seed, like a garment with a patch on it, like a sower, like a group of waiting servants, and many others.

But, what is the kingdom?

Sometimes the evangelists speak of the Kingdom as present, sometimes as in the future. How can it have past, present and future aspects? How can it be something that has been realized, something that is being realized, and something that will be realized? For, in Jesus' teaching, the kingdom had come, was in the process of coming and would come.

So we have two sets of threes: (1) three contexts for the words of Jesus: in Roman Palestine to Israel; in the world of the Christian believer of the first century; in our twenty-first century context. (2) three meanings of 'the Kingdom," past present and future.

Now it's obvious that wherever we are and whenever we live we think in such terms. We think about our past, about our present and about our future.

The Gospels relate all of time to the Kingdom of God. It is a very rich concept then. Basically it means 'reign,' 'rule,' 'sovereignty.' The Kingdom of God means that God rules as King. The Kingdom of God is the sphere of God's rule, where he rules. God is ruler of his people, of his world, of the universe. But, is there a common theme to his sovereignty? We can find it in the fact that God is manifesting his sovereignty over the evil that is in the world.

So God's kingdom is in the world in the people of God who also are looking for a decisive future manifestation of God's sovereignty. God was going to act in the coming of Messiah and in the apocalyptic upheavals by which God would introduce the new world order at the end of this one. They were expecting it urgently at the time of Jesus.

Jesus announced that the kingdom of God had come. Not now in the older Jewish sense. Not in the sense that most of his contemporaries hoped for. God's power is now operating in a new way in the world, said Jesus. The Kingdom of God has come (*Matthew* 12:28, *Luke* 1120, *Mark* 1:14-15). When the disciples are sent on their mission during Jesus' ministry, they are to declare that the Kingdom of God has come (*Luke* 10:9-11. *Matthew* 12:28, *Luke* 11:20). The powers of the world to come are present with the coming of Jesus. The kingdom of God is here. God's kingdom is now being revealed on earth. It is a dramatic announcement. So it is a time of crisis. His hearers must now make a choice. They must take sides. They will in their decision show themselves to be wise or foolish, faithful or unfaithful. The time of crisis is now. They will show whether they are prepared for the things that will happen as Jesus' ministry proceeds.

The time passes. Decisions are taken and in the course of events, Jesus, he who proclaimed the coming of the Kingdom, the good news, was now himself proclaimed as the Agent of God's new act. He was now the 'Son of man,' who would return to the earth to complete the purpose of God in creation.

So there are parables whose purpose is to encourage watchfulness and preparedness for the Second Advent of Christ.

We know how the early preachers spoke about this. They said that it would be like a thief in the night (*1 Thessalonians* 5:28). They warned that, in view of the expected event, they should be wakeful, ready (*Mark* 21:34-36). For the Gospels have come out of the experience of the early church, as well as out of Judaea and Galilee.

So the parables are now set in a new context. It is the context of the anticipation of the early church. The first-century church at first waited for the Second Coming of Christ with eager expectation. A decade passes, and another, and another. The believers now began to realise that it has not taken place as they had hoped. By the time of the writing of the Gospels, it was well on into the latter half of the century. That the Advent had not taken place coloured their thinking. They interpreted the parables, and Jesus teaching as a whole, in the light of the fact that the Advent had not taken place. Their disappointment and realization of the fact, is the milieu in which we are to read what they wrote.

In that important respect — whatever else the differences — their contexts and that context of present-day Adventism is similar. Indeed the similarity is quite striking. The Gospels had a very important message for them. Since it did, it has a similar message for today's disappointed Adventists.

So we can pass to the third context.

Take the parable of the talents. One commentator observed: 'The whole parable becomes an announcement and confirmation of the delay of the *parousia*.' A man goes away on a journey. Before he does he given monies to his servants. He stays away a considerable time. 'After a long time the master of those servants came and settled accounts with them. In Luke's version a particular reason is given for Jesus telling this parable. 'He proceeded to tell a parable . . . because they supposed that the Kingdom of God was to appear immediately' (*Luke* 19:11). Now, put the parable in the setting of the church's expectation of the soon Advent and it has an immediate and very telling point. Remember, too, that Luke was writing with the Gentile church in particular in mind.

The master's return is the *parousia*, the Advent. So Luke applies the parable to the new context where it has a real bite in relation to the experienced delay of the *parousia*. So does Matthew. In so doing, he included a piece of warning, exhortation. Be occupied in making good use of the resources you've been entrusted with in the waiting time. Simple as that. But so appropriate!

Take the parable of the waiting servants as told by Luke (12:35-38) and (*Mark* 13:33-37), who focuses upon the doorkeeper. Again the parable is brilliant in its simplicity. A householder is to return from the wedding feast at some undisclosed time during the night. While the night watches pass (the dawn is becoming closer) those servants are ready who are awake and watching. The addition of the coming of the thief gives rise to the comment that the householder would not have left his house had he known precisely when the thief would have come.

The division of the night, the night watches, are a symbol of the passing of time. Luke portrays one watch passing, then another, and another. He is suggesting the experience of the church as decade after decade passed and the Advent did not take place. The admonition is quite clear. Do not be in distress! Wait patiently, however long the time of waiting. Hold fast to the tasks in hand and wait in hope.

The reference to the thief is an allusion to the future. Take account of the Day of the Lord, for it will be sudden. The Advent, when it comes, will be sudden.

What constituted appropriate warning and admonition to Jesus' disciples in view of the events about to take place, now in the new context, takes on a new but very appropriate meaning in the new situation of the church's disappointment. Expectation can't be kept at a pitch of enthusiasm as weary decades pass. As one observer remarked, what happened in the first century church was that the expectations, buoyant and vivid at first, hardened into a dogma. That has happened since too. What was needed then was a message of encouragement to keep faith, to keep going, and to continue in the life of faith, hope and the performance of the tasks at hand.

But there is more to be said. Indeed, there is. In the teaching of the New Testament, the Kingdom of God is not identical with the Second Advent. So we can hope for the Kingdom of God while disappointed about the Second Advent. For the Kingdom comes and comes and comes again. The passing generations of the faithful are part of the Kingdom, active in promoting it and responsive in the cooperating with God who is its Creator. We pray, 'Thy kingdom come!' and that prayer is fulfilled as we take up the tasks of this day and of every day and perform them with dedication, diligence and with hope. An important aspect of the teaching of the parable is that the disciple is a servant. A feature of the servant is that he is humble.

But the New Testament allows us sometimes to identify the Kingdom of God with the Second Advent as the means by which the reign of God is finally established, the means by which human history comes to its end and God fulfills his purpose. It is the great 'Day of the Lord' because it introduces and leads to God's eternal reign.

This close *association of future and present* is such a striking feature of Jesus' teaching and of the New Testament expressions of hope.

We can isolate one aspect and play down the other. We can stack our cards toward the future and let *expectation* shape our life. Or we can focus on the present and de-emphasise *fulfillment*. There are corresponding consequences when one emphasis becomes virtually exclusive. But if we emphasise fulfillment in the present life of faith, we shall be able to handle the future. An eschatology realised in the present brings satisfaction, whereas expected but unrealised eschatology always leaves room for possible doubt and discouragement. And always stands in danger of becoming a dogma.

So we return to the parables.

The important element in each context is that we are in a time of waiting. However it has come about, we're in the waiting time. Whatever the other circumstances, we are waiting for something we expect. And in each case, we don't know when it will happen.

The time of waiting is a time of activity. The time of waiting *is* the time of fulfillment. If the future Kingdom of God is continuous with the fulfillment in the present, then 'soon' is 'now' and it could not be any sooner than that. What could be — to put it so— more present than the Kingdom of God, God's rule, realised in the heart of the believer? Part of that realization consists in hope. But how that hope is to be fulfilled is not in our hands, but in the hands of the God in whom we trust.

Now we apply the parables to our own modern context. For Adventists this means we take into account a situation similar to that of first-century Christians. They came to terms with their disappointment. Adventists are coming to terms with theirs.

One way would be to turn the Second Advent into a dogma. We must keep it as an important doctrine, reinterpret the notion of 'soon' so that we apply it to our present experience and get on with the tasks of the present. But it does not have to become a dogma to let us concentrate on the present. Both things happened in the early days of the church, as did a third. The teaching of the Second Advent was interpreted was subordinate to the promptings, the admonition, the incentives to which reflection and expectation of the Advent gave rise. There was no need to think of it as *literally* imminent. But act as if it were. And as — in the long ;centuries of the experience of the church, the initial expectation of the apostolic believers became more and more remote, receding more and more into the past, the church occupied itself with the tasks of the day, and where faithful to its calling, addressed itself to the needs of the community and of the world, developing its teaching as it did so.

All the while the church prayed, 'Thy Kingdom come!' It was ready as it addressed itself to present tasks for whatever would happen and however God would act in the coming days.

Finally, we turn to the parable of the waiting virgins. They expect the bridegroom to return to his father's house with his bride. There has been a delay. Perhaps it has to do with the marriage settlement. It is possible that such could occur, that the bridegroom be delayed until midnight. The 'foolish virgins' were short-sighted. Why? They did not consider that the bridegroom might be delayed. But they were waiting. They wanted to be ready. But you can't easily get a lamp lit quickly, and it does not take long for a person to enter a house, just a few moments. So there is a message for different contexts. There may be sudden crisis. Even though there has been a delay in what is expected. Be ready for it. 'The readiness is all.'

So it was in Jesus' day.

So it was in the time of the early church.

So it is now, for the church that awaits the Kingdom of God.

V 'Lesser Light to Greater Light'?
How do the writings of E. G. White relate to the Scriptures?

The answer the author herself gave was: 'as **the** lesser light to the greater light'. It is this answer we shall try to understand.

For the Adventist the corpus of the White writings is not to be considered as one to be chosen among others (and there are many others) for the function of understanding Scripture. It is not just a lesser light. It is the lesser light. Others are not given such status or even recognised. Once embraced, the believer does not realise what is lost by ignoring other sources. Unfortunately, such an attitude leads to unnecessary and unwanted problems.

What sort of images does this metaphorical connection between lights conjure up? What could it mean as 'light' gets referred to two bodies of writing? Certainly the intention is not that the lesser light moves to the remote background when the greater light has been discovered through its instrumentality. But it seems that it expresses the idea that Adventists want it to register. To put it naively: Read E .G. White and you will be led to the understanding of the Bible, from the lesser to the greater understanding. That is what the word 'to' suggests. There is to be movement from the one, subsidiary, to the other, primary. So on a basic level we may simply take it to mean that the lesser will assist the believer in reading Scripture, as suggestions are made about the meanings of this or that passage.

But there is another significant meaning of the phrase. The lesser will suggest how the Scriptures are to be much more widely interpreted. The lesser will recommend the fruitful way of approaching Scripture so as to produce its overall teaching and establish doctrine for the community. We focus on this second approach. The concern is with interpretation to establish doctrine and, for the Adventist, how to interpret 'prophecy'.

It is both a claim and a warning.

The claim is that both make demands for understanding and response. The warning is that the basic authentic independent authority is that of the Bible. The 'lesser' is a derived authority, and should therefore not be given the primary attention and respect.

The warning is relevant when and where more volume, time and attention is given to the lesser and so makes it in practice primary. That this is the case in terms of volume is obvious. Evidence of this is to be found as the Adventist believer, when searching for meaning, accepts the subsidiary writing as primary. Consider the sheer volume of the lesser writings, the publicity given to them, and their relative simplicity. Take into account the production of new editions and productions of the 'lesser' writings, added to the constant insistence that here is where guidance is to be found for solution of problems and for personal guidance over many areas of life, personal, ecclesiastical and social. When the writings expound a biblical text, the interpretation is taken as settling the matter.

If for example a New Testament specialist, or someone with knowledge of the Greek text, suggests another understanding than the one expressed in the text of the 'lesser', the likely response often received is that E. G. White says this, i.e. something different, and that is the end of the matter.

The attractive fact is that the 'lesser' writings are easily accessible. The language is simple and is readily understood. So it is easily read and that makes it attractive. The biblical writings often demand real effort to be understood. That is often beyond the competence and interests of the believer in the pew and, sad to say, many in the pulpit. Should you ask, 'Tell me what is the message of the book of Jeremiah?', or 'Please explain to me the teaching of the book of Romans' or please explain what the Bible teaches about immortality, or about creation, you will probably get an unwelcome or unsatisfactory answer in the light of the emphatic professed claim to the importance of Scripture. When it comes to understanding the Scriptures, the task of interpretation is often very demanding indeed. It is much easier to lift and employ an established method of interpretation from a secondary source and take it as needing no qualification.

Now let us consider the way the claim is expressed, as 'a lesser light to lead to the greater' the greater being the Scriptures. A Protestant claim is that the Scripture as it is read delivers its meaning to the sincere reader. That is the basic meaning of *scriptura sola*, sometimes rendered as 'the Bible and the Bible only.' The Reformers meant by this that no intermediary was needed for the basic Christian understanding of the Scripture. Scripture was the means to faith and provided the means for sustaining that faith. When the ploughboy read Scripture, now so recently translated into his own tongue, he would understand it. There was no need for secondary sources. He could find faith as he read.

The fact that Scripture is interpreted must be given due weight. As it is read, on any level, it gets interpreted. So there is a further meaning to be considered. The 'lesser light' may then be seen as providing the decisive suggestion as to how Scripture should be rightly interpreted. It provides what basic approach should be taken to arrive at a fruitful way of understanding the Bible. How shall we interpret the Bible? The 'spirit of prophecy' (an accepted title for the White writings) provides the answer.

The answer given to that question, the understanding that leads to a fruitful answer is quite clear. Interpret the message of Scripture as a story. Draw evidence from Scripture for the stages in that story. It begins in the heavenly sphere where myriads of supernatural beings, all creations of God, are in conflict. The outcome of this celestial conflict is that the rebels are duly excluded from the heaven of the faithful creatures, those who remain loyal to the demands of God, and as in John Milton's *Paradise Lost* the rebels are excluded from the presence of God, but after the creation of man, they have access to the human creatures, some who in their turn fail to fulfill God's demands. So 'the great controversy' continues: God, the creator, the source of all good, versus Satan, the embodiment of rebellion and the source of all evil. To produce this understanding, the emphasis is on carefully selected passages of Scripture, including apocalyptic. These are to take pride of place for serious attention. An obvious interest and attention is given to the apocalyptic passages of Scripture to a serious neglect of other kinds of 'writing'. So, for example, it is the apocalyptic passages selected from the Gospels that are put in a very different context from the original one and served to establish doctrine. A main source is the book of Revelation.

The story emphasises last day events, the presently occurring and the coming judgment, investigative and executive, and ends with the punishment of the wicked and the literal salvation of the righteous. After the bloodletting, human history ends with the restoration (?) of the original state: i.e. acknowledgement of God's sovereignty and justice.

Enthusiastic recourse to symbolic passages, taken as literally prophetic, provides hope for the believer encouraged along the sad course of human history, and especially for the few, who at the end of that history constitute a faithful 'remnant' and who with the resurrected redeemed of the ages inherit the kingdom of heaven. So with this help from the 'lesser light' we are invited to take this story as the clue to the interpretation of the Scripture. So the 'greater light' in made to shine in a very restricted way. There is a further important consideration. E. G. White often did not understand the debates that were to lead to decisions about doctrine. On the other hand she was emphatic when endorsing teachings and approaches of which she approved. Since she was accepted as divine authority, these then became widely established within the emerging community.

The important example that was widely accepted was her attitude to the modified idea of 'sanctuary', this received primary attention after the Great Disappointment and fostered hope in the emerging community. The idea of sanctuary and cleansing, retained from the preaching of William Miller, now became the key to the accepted method of interpretation, and received elaborate and complex treatment, but put in a new context from that of Miller, received a revolutionary treatment following the lead of Hiram Edison.

The images of light seem to suggest that there is to be movement from one body of writings to a move from the lesser to the greater. What is of some interest is the phrasing of the assertion: 'lesser to greater' rather than 'dimmer to brighter'. Here it is not the features of light that are the basis of the contrast. We shall not comment further on this interesting observation. Simply ask, 'What does the unique phrase say that Scripture has but that the 'spirit of prophecy' does not?'

So we turn back to mid-nineteenth-century Miller's hermeneutic. Adventism emerges as Millerite apocalypticism becomes radically revised. But it retained its determined respect for an unquestionable and exclusive heritage of prophetic interpretation. But it lacked later the serious and extended debate that was a feature of the earlier activity from which the doctrinal tradition emerged. It insisted on acceptance of the hermeneutic method and the results it produced as orthodox. It is now simply not seriously discussed by orthodox Adventism.

So, what is the answer to the question in our subtitle? How do the writings of E. G. White relate to the Scriptures?

The 'spirit of prophecy', the title given to the White body of writings, endorsed both the results of the methods of interpreting Scripture, adopted by the early Adventists, namely the employment of the two ideas:

(1) of a cosmic supernatural conflict, the 'great controversy' and its tragic consequences when it gets transplanted into the world of humans, when the story becomes human history;

(2) of the elaborate reinterpretation of the idea of the 'cleansing of the sanctuary' inherited from William Miller, now an activity in heavenly spheres. The sanctuary is in heaven. There is no parallel activity on earth. However its results concern all earth's inhabitants.

These ideas become the accepted basis for the prophetic reinterpretation of Scripture, and the establishing of Adventist doctrine. The emphasis is on God's justice and his activity as judge, on the events initiated in 'heaven' that produced evil also in the human creation, and so required a demonstration of that justice. At the end, after a long process of examination of the human creatures, judgment is to be executed on the inhabitants of earth, as well upon celestial creatures who initiated and perpetuated evil and upon the arch enemy, Satan. The result is that after the great purge by fire, one pulse of harmony beats through the whole creation. God is vindicated. Evil and sin is forever destroyed. God's justice is satisfied.

To refer to the symbols of light employed: The lesser light endorsed the hermeneutic method: the central employment of the ideas of the Great Controversy and Cleansing of the Sanctuary as providing a structure and producing an elaborate system of doctrine. The lesser light also endorsed the actual teachings its method produced. It was thus instrumental in establishing the pillar teachings of Adventism that continue to be accepted as the church's norm and that identify the church as 'the people of prophecy'.

Ellen White wrote:

'Little heed is given to the Bible, and the Lord has given a lesser light to lead men and women to the greater light . . . . The gift was given not for a rule of faith, but for the comfort of his people, and to correct those who err from Bible truth.'

'I recommend to you, dear reader, the Word of God as the rule of your faith and practice. By that Word we are to be judged. God has, in that Word, promised to give visions in the last day, not for a new rule of faith, but for the comfort of his people and to correct those who err from Bible truth.[7]

---

7   'Review and Herald', Jan. 20 1903, p. 15, *Early Writings*, p. 78.

That is equivalent to saying that the gift, in correcting you, will lead you back to the rule of faith! She did not see the paradox she has stated! These eschatological teachings have, in fact, become the rule of faith, the primary emphasis in traditional Adventism.

VI Hiram Edson's' Hypothesis

Hiram Edson wrote the following about his experience on October 23rd, 1844, the day after the Great Disappointment.

> 'Heaven seemed open to my view and I saw distinctly and clearly that instead of our High Priest coming out of the Most Holy of the holiest to come to this earth on the tenth day of the seventh month at the end of the 2,300 days, he for the first time entered on that day the second apartment and that he had a work to perform in the Most Holy before coming to this earth. That he came to the marriage supper at that time (as mentioned in the parable of the Ten Virgins). In other words, to the Ancient of Days to receive a kingdom, dominion and glory and we must wait for his return from the wedding.[8]

---

8   We now analyse briefly each of the several key terms in Edson's statement.

The picture that the seeming of the opening sentence of heaven suggests is of the clouds, seen at first immediately above being dissipated. We take this to suggest that what was unclear and obscure now is now becoming clear. But the serious question is: What sort of reality is this? What does a psychological condition have to do with reality? What may be claimed on the basis of the experience? An interpretation is called for. Edson is not at any loss in supplying one. He interprets what he seems to see in the terms of his already firm convictions. He assumes that his audience will know what he intends by speaking of 'our High Priest' and 'second apartment' without further explanation. Then follow a series of technical terms: 'tenth day', 'seventh month', 'second apartment' 'most holy'. These terms are clear only with elaborate explanation, requiring a detailed knowledge of the sanctuary, or temple ritual and procedures. What he takes for granted is the assumption that these are the ones directly relevant and fitting the inquirer to discern the meaning of the 'vision'. The idea that gave meaning to this is that the believer must think of the heavenly, the transcendent, in terms relevant to the earthly Jewish sanctuary. The language is very familiar to the disappointed Adventist, if not to the present reader.

This is an elaborate statement, set firmly within the context of the puzzled believers, and using the only vocabulary he knew. In Edson's account the actual terms of the original text are not used, but the underlying idea is retained and given an interpretation which renders a quite different understanding to the phrase 'then shall the sanctuary be cleansed'. What is important is that he retains the date set for the expected event, 1844, even if he does not mention it. The interpretation hinges on that fact. This becomes an intrinsic element in Adventist dogma for the future and is retained still in the present. That is a remarkable fact. It involves endorsing the method and some conclusions of William Miller.

The speculation is about proposed events in 'heaven'. It is an idea that gives rise to Edson's state of mind and to renewed hope. For him the 'vision' provides confirmation of his idea. That was an attitude to visions shared among many of his contemporary believers. The hope is of a soon return after the proposed ministry in the Most Holy. There are hints that when the group had accepted the new idea, its members thought that there would not be a long wait. Two items suggest this. 1. Edson himself had proposed that 'the time of the end' began in 1798, a point then already several

---

Attention now turns to the heavenly ritual. The account employs a mixture of metaphors. The 'marriage supper' and 'receiving of a kingdom' are associated with the outcome. When the 'marriage supper' ends the high priest returns from the 'wedding'. Quite a series of figures are correlated here, based on selected portions of Scripture interpreted as symbols of crucial events. It is all is rather vague, picturesque and puzzling exegesis. But whatever he performs must be done before the expected end will occur. No hint is given as to how long that will be!

Final comments The High Priest is none other than the resurrected, ascended Jesus. These two processes, resurrection and ascension precede further activity, 'ascent' relocation for the heavenly ministry. We need an explanation of the actual priestly activity.

For further discussion of Edson's reported statement see the materials available on the Internet under Hiram Edson.

decades in the past. 2. Also, on several occasions E. G. White made the confident prediction[9] that some in her audience would be alive and be present at the Advent, i.e. when the 'bridegroom', the High Priest, returned to earth. While the hope that there would not be a long extension of the waiting time served to buoy up the group's spirits in the immediate days following the Disappointment. After decades of non-fulfillment there are now serious problems to be faced.

The crucial idea is of an ongoing activity in the newly postulated 'heavenly sanctuary'. That idea provides the grounds for renewed hope. The 'prophecy' discerned in the book of *Daniel* can be given new life, although with one big difference from the former understanding. There can be no confirmation for it in the present. But if the last events do not happen as anticipated as the heavenly ministration comes to its end, no one will ever know whether the conviction is true. If the prediction of the course of events is false, it cannot be known.

Basic to all of this is the acceptance of a particular speculation about the Bible, as Scripture. This is an interpretation of the inspiration of the writings. It's a twofold speculation leading to an assertion that inspiration grounds the authority of Scripture on the one hand, and on the other insists that since established as authoritative the sentences of Scripture, are to be taken as literally true and so when interpreted the doctrine that results has divine authority. The result of such speculation is an assertion of the undeniable authority of Scripture and also the teaching derived from it.

We take a further example from Edson's enthusiastic prophetic speculation and with it raise the question, How is it possible to justify the tortuous generation of sanctuary hermeneutic involved with Hiram Edson's treatment, a literalism that finds symbols and then interprets them in an eccentric 'prophetic' manner. Below, we take as example how the repeated occurrence of the word 'time' is

---

9   Spoken at the Conference, Battle Creek, Michigan, May 1856 and on several other occasions.

made the basis for an elaborate and fantastic speculation. This illustrates the persuasive post-excitement mentality of the disappointed but hopeful emerging community, each giving support to the other, but all the while awaiting revelations from God. Their attitude was the following. We shall retain the hermeneutic even if it led to Disappointment and in this way shall save it. It has more to do, much more! We save the situation as we save and apply the same hermeneutic that has this far produced only disappointment. So we reinterpret in spite of the warning of the immediately experienced events. In hope we reinterpret using the same method of interpretation, 'prophetic interpretation' that led to the Disappointment. Such interpretation demands that we focus on certain concepts to the neglect of others, and on interpreting the key concepts in a particular and questionable way. Certain words are key. These are used to experiment (so to speak) with exegesis in hope of getting a positive result.

The task is to produce a persuasive post-excitement post-disappointment mentality. The Great Disappointment of 1844 led to reappraisal on the part of those who had expected the coming of Christ but whose hopes had been dashed. The attitude is not to abandon everything, but to construct a future for faith. The aim is to save the situation and at the same time to save the hermeneutic which produced the disappointment. Go on re-interpreting with the same method in spite of the severe warning of the Disappointment, that is to say in spite of the previous error it produced. Abandon the result, but not the method. In doing so await the revelation from God and be assured of receiving genuine divine guidance with the same certainty that assured believers that Miller was divinely guided. So it comes to pass that Edson and his companions justify the tortuous generation of sanctuary hermeneutic. Two words are central, 'sanctuary' and 'time'.

I was very much astonished as I read his comments on *Leviticus* 26, and observed his extreme fascination with the word 'time'. He made an inexcusably grammatical mistake, He did not discern the difference between the meaning of (1) 'time' as denoting a particular period, and (2) 'time' as expressing succession as in the phrase 'for the second time', 'for the last time'. He lumps the repeated terms together and makes an aggregate of 'seven times' as a result. Thereon hangs his tale.

Taking 'time' to mean 'year', taking 'year' to mean 360 days, taking a day to mean a year, from 'seven times' he deduces a period of 2250 years. Since there are, he finds, seven prophetic 'times' in the chapter, this means 2520 years (7 times 360 = 2520). The community encourage him in his search to provide an interpretation. He submits to the 'examination and inspection of the brethren.' They await and will hopefully endorse his conclusions. That is how results follow and are accepted as divine truth.

Edson wrote a long series of articles which he called 'The times of the gentiles, and the deliverance and restoration of the remnant of Israel from the seven times, or 2520 years of Assyrian or pagan and papal captivity considered.'

He claimed that the 1844 date was 'uninvalidated', but did not explain why. He took it for granted. Then gave an elaborate and very lengthy treatment of the above subject. Basing his reasoning on his reading of *Leviticus* 26 he finds that the 2520 years begin in 723 B.C. with the imprisonment of King Hoshea and so end with a final date in A.D. 1798 with the downfall of the papacy, the saints thereby being delivered from the papal power. So begin the 'time of the end' with its continuing hope that it will not be too long!

Edson shows no interest at all in the picture of the God displayed in the chapter but is obsessed with the urge to find material that can be extracted for purposes of prophecy. Such neglect involves serious failure of discernment. He misses the basic understanding, in this case of a God threatening to punish in real history, the history of the Hebrew people.

One wonders whether this hermeneutic is what Froom and his followers are so concerned to defend. Notice how one speculative system leads to another.

One speculative system, fundamentalism, is a particular understanding of biblical inspiration as ground for biblical authority. This coupled with a literalist interpretation of the symbolic text. A second speculative system, a prophetic system when itself duly modified provided the means for a third resultant speculative system, the millennial eschatology with its intricate detail of concern with probation, investigative judgment, and final punishment and reward and in its reference to history employs the 'day for a year' principle.

What dominates in the system we have discussed is a basic principle: God is judge inactive judgment. The conception of God as judge, in judgment, dominates it.

www.ingramcontent.com/pod-product-compliance
Lightning Source LLC
Chambersburg PA
CBHW031451070426
42452CB00038B/791